EASY
FRENCH
DISHES

COOKING AROUND THE WORLD

EASY
FRENCH
DISHES

SAFEWAY/GOOD HOUSEKEEPING

COOKERY NOTES

All spoon measures are level unless otherwise stated.

Size 2 eggs should be used except when otherwise stated.

Granulated sugar is used unless otherwise stated.

The oven should be preheated to the required temperature unless otherwise stated.

Published exclusively for
Safeway
6 Millington Road, Hayes, Middlesex UB3 4AY
by Ebury Press
A division of Random House
20 Vauxhall Bridge Road
London SW1V 2SA

First published 1994

Edited by Julia Canning and Louise Steele
Recipes by Good Housekeeping Institute and Linda Frazer
Designed by Behram Kapadia
Photography by Michelle Garrett
Food stylist Liz Trigg

The paper in this book is acid-free

Typeset by Textype Typesetters, Cambridge
Printed in Italy

ISBN 0-09-182499-0

CONTENTS

FOREWORD

Welcome to *Easy French Dishes*, part of the exciting new *Cooking Around the World* series produced in association with Safeway.

Each of the six books in this unique series is dedicated to one of the countries of the world most renowned for its mouthwatering cuisine. All the recipes have been double tested by the cooks in the Good Housekeeping Institute using Safeway's quality produce.

Presented in a clear, step-by-step format, many of the recipes are quick and easy enough to suit the hectic pace of modern living, although anyone looking to create an exotic feast for a really special occasion will not be disappointed.

To take the 'worry factor' out of using new ingredients, you will find tips on how to identify, select and prepare exotic fruit and vegetables, aromatic herbs and spices and other produce in the introductory pages.

Through the *Cooking Around the World* series you can bring the tastes and flavours of six fascinating countries to your table.

MOYRA FRASER
Cookery Editor
Good Housekeeping

INTRODUCTION

The French are renowned for their gourmet cooking and the secret of their success lies in the attention paid to the freshness and quality of ingredients and to the care in preparation of food. Once you have mastered these basic principles, cooking French-style is easy.

The range of ingredients featured in French cooking is huge, varying from superb creamy cheeses and luxurious shellfish to pungent herbs, luscious soft fruit and, of course, excellent wines. The style of cooking varies from region to region to produce a stunning range of both sweet and savoury dishes that are admired throughout the world.

HERBS

Both fresh and dried herbs are used extensively in French cooking as flavourings, notably in salad dressings and sauces.

BOUQUET GARNI is a bunch of mixed herbs which are tied together or wrapped in muslin so that they can be removed from a dish once they have infused flavour into the cooked ingredients. The most popular combination of herbs consists of a bay leaf, a sprig of thyme and three sprigs of parsley – but you can vary the herbs as you wish.

CHIVES with their delicate onion flavour, are especially good in salads. Finely chopped, they are often sprinkled over a dish as a garnish.

ROSEMARY The strong sweet scent of this herb combines excellently with lamb dishes.

THYME grows abundantly in the wild and is frequently used to flavour soups and stews.

BASIL An aromatic herb, basil is used a great deal in the south of France to add character to savoury dishes. It has a particular affinity with tomatoes.

CHERVIL looks a little like parsley, but has a very strong aromatic flavour which goes well with egg dishes, cream soups and salads.

TARRAGON has a mild aniseed flavour and is excellent with chicken, fish and for flavouring vinegar.

FINES HERBES This is a traditional French blend of four herbs – parsley, chervil, tarragon and chives. Use finely chopped to sprinkle over salads, omelettes and chicken or fish dishes.

CHEESE

Cheese is a natural accompaniment to wine and during a meal in France it is served as a separate course after the main savoury dish. Almost every village in France has its own speciality cheese, so as a country France offers a huge choice of cheeses with different flavours and textures. There are certain types which are now very familiar in this country.

BRIE This distinctive cheese, with its large flat round shape, is a soft creamy cheese with an edible chalky rind. Young Brie has a firm, almost crumbly texture, while riper Brie has a stronger flavour and an almost runny texture.

CAMEMBERT is a small round flat cheese, sold whole or in foil-wrapped sections in a wooden box. It has a velvety edible rind and a smooth soft yellow texture inside with a mild fruity flavour.

CHEVRE is goat's cheese and there are many different varieties available, ranging from the soft fresh spreadable variety to the hard dried type. It is often served lightly grilled with a salad.

FROMAGE FRAIS A fresh soft cheese, fromage frais has a variable fat content depending on whether it is made with whole or skimmed milk. It has a very creamy texture and makes an excellent substitute for yogurt in both sweet and savoury dishes.

ROQUEFORT is perhaps the best known of all the French blue cheeses. It has a distinctive nutty flavour with a creamy, crumbly texture streaked with green veins. It is particularly good served with dessert wines or crumbled into sauces and dressings.

PATES AND TERRINES

France has the most variety of pâtés and terrines of any country in the world. Made from fish, meat or poultry, pâtés are served either at the beginning of a meal as an hors d'oeuvre or with fresh French bread as a snack. Terrines are traditionally cooked in earthenware dishes and are sometimes turned out for serving. One of the most famous French pâtés is Pâté de Foie Gras. This is made from goose liver, which is extremely expensive and regarded as a great delicacy.

SALADS

The French love salad and will serve it as a starter or as a course on its own or with cheese after the main course. Green salads are made up of a great variety of lettuce, the most popular being lamb's lettuce, frisé, rocket and radiccio. **VINAIGRETTE,** often referred to as French Dressing, is the classic dressing for salads. It is generally made with one part wine vinegar to three parts olive oil, and flavourings, such as mustard, sugar, fresh herbs and garlic, are often added. It is essential to whisk the dressing thoroughly before serving.

GARLIC AND SHALLOTS

Both garlic and shallots are essential ingredients in French cooking. Garlic is used extensively as a flavouring in both savoury hot dishes and salads. Shallots are a member of the onion family but they are smaller than onions and have a more pointed shape. Their delicate and distinctive flavour has made them a classic ingredient for many French sauces.

MUSTARD

Mustard is used to give a distinctive flavour to all manner of French savoury dishes. The best known varieties are Dijon – pale and pungent; Bordeaux – dark and mild flavoured; and Moutarde de Meaux – a grainy mustard, often sold in grey stoneware jars.

CREME FRAICHE

Used in much the same way as cream, crème fraîche is a traditional French ingredient. A cross between yogurt and cream, it is slightly acidic without being sour and is a delicious addition to both savoury and sweet dishes.

WINES AND SPIRITS IN COOKING

Alcohol is used extensively in French cooking to give richness, succulence and flavour to all manner of dishes. Generally red wines are used with game and the darker meats, and white wines with fish, poultry, veal and pork, although the classic Coq au Vin does, in fact, include red Burgundy wine among its ingredients.

Brandies, spirits and liqueurs are used to flambé (flame) dishes. During this process the actual alcohol is burned off and only the flavour remains to give special richness to the dish.

Meat, poultry and fish are frequently marinated before cooking in a mixture of wine or liqueur and other flavourings (such as herbs, garlic, lemon rind) for anything from a few minutes to several hours or overnight, and in some cases even longer. This marinating process helps tenderise and flavour the food and the liquid is often used finally to baste foods during cooking or to make a sauce for serving.

Macerating foods in alcohol is the technique applied when fruits (whether dried, fresh or glacéed) are left to soften and plump out in a spirit of liqueur for a length of time before draining off or cooking in the alcohol, according to the recipe.

STARTERS

Start meals on a stylish note with dishes drawn from the very heart of the French kitchen. Here you will find a selection of gastronomic delicacies which look and taste wonderful, and are easy to create. Dishes range from the classic elegance of sole mousselines to a tasty liver pâté, given a new twist with the flavours of lemon and almonds. Mouthwatering pastry cases filled with creamy crab or asparagus make lightweight entrées, as well as excellent accompaniments to drinks, while deep-fried camembert served with a tangy rhubarb sauce typifies the imaginative flair of French cooking.

OPPOSITE
LEFT Crab Bouchées
RIGHT Crème St Germaine Soup

CREME ST GERMAINE SOUP

SERVES 6–8

1 small cos lettuce, washed and shredded
6 salad onions, sliced
450 g (1 lb) frozen peas
2-3 sprigs of mint
1.5 lt (2½ pt) chicken stock
25 g (1 oz) butter
2 × 15 ml tbs plain flour
salt and pepper
3 × 15 ml tbs double cream
sprigs of mint, to garnish

1 Place the lettuce, salad onions, peas, mint sprigs and 1.2 lt (2 pt) of the stock in a large saucepan and bring to the boil. Reduce the heat and simmer for 20 minutes, until the peas are very tender. Remove the mint from the pan and blend the soup in a food processor until smooth, then pass through a sieve.

2 Melt the butter in the rinsed out pan, stir in the flour and cook over a low heat for 1 minute. Stir in the soup, bring to the boil and cook, stirring, until thickened slightly. Leave to cool, stirring occasionally, then chill for at least 3 hours.

3 Just before serving, adjust seasoning to taste and add a little extra stock if necessary to make a thin soup. Pour the soup into bowls and swirl in the cream. Garnish each bowl of soup with a sprig of mint.

GARLIC SOUP WITH CRISPY CROUTES

SERVES 6

5 × 15 ml tbs olive oil
20 garlic cloves, skinned
1.2 lt (2 pt) chicken or vegetable stock
salt and pepper
2 eggs, separated
about 12 small, thin slices stale bread
4 × 15 ml tbs single cream (optional)
chopped fresh parsley, to garnish

1 Heat 3 × 15 ml tbs oil in a saucepan, add the garlic, cover and cook gently for about 10 minutes until softened and tinged with colour. Add the stock, season with salt and pepper and simmer for 20 minutes.

2 Meanwhile, lightly whisk the egg whites. Place the bread on a baking tray and spread with the egg white. Bake at 200°C/400°F/Gas Mark 6 for 6-7 minutes. Divide the croûtes between six flat soup bowls and keep warm.

3 Sieve the soup into a clean pan. Beat the egg yolks with the remaining oil and cream, if using. Stir in a little of the soup. Return the soup to the pan and heat gently, stirring all the time, until the soup begins to thicken slightly. Do not let it boil.

4 Adjust the seasoning. Pour the soup over the croûtes to serve and garnish with parsley.

Garlic Soup with Crispy Croûtes

SALMON RILLETTES

SERVES 8

335 g (12 oz) fresh salmon fillets, skinned
salt and pepper
150 g (5 oz) butter, softened
50 g (2 oz) onion or shallots, skinned and chopped
115 ml (4 fl oz) dry white wine
115 g (4 oz) smoked salmon, roughly chopped
2 × 15 ml tbs olive oil
4 × 5 ml tsp lemon juice
pinch of ground nutmeg
sprigs of flat-leaf parsley, to garnish

1 Place the salmon fillets on a plate, sprinkle with salt and leave to stand for about 30 minutes. Rinse, drain and dry the fish.

2 Heat 25 g (1 oz) butter in a medium frying pan, add the onion or shallots and cook gently for 5 minutes until softened. Add the fresh salmon, pour the wine over, cover and cook gently for about 4 minutes, or until the fish is tender and cooked. Lift it out of the pan and flake the fish, then leave it to cool. Meanwhile, boil the cooking liquid to reduce it to 3-4 × 15 ml tbs. Leave to cool.

3 Place the fresh salmon, onion mixture, the smoked salmon and 75 g (3 oz) butter in a blender or food processor. Blend until the ingredients are roughly mixed. Add the oil, lemon juice, nutmeg and season with salt and pepper. Blend again until the ingredients are well mixed but still retain some texture. Adjust the seasoning, if necessary. Spoon the fish mixture into a small upright terrine, leaving 1-2.5 cm (½-1 in) headspace for the clarified butter. Cover tightly and chill for at least 30 minutes, or until firm to the touch.

4 Melt the remaining butter. Remove from the heat and, with a small metal spoon, remove all scum from the surface. Decorate the salmon mixture with sprigs of flat-leaf parsley and spoon over the clarified butter to completely cover the surface. Cover with a lid and refrigerate for 2-3 days.

LEMON AND ALMOND LIVER PATE

SERVES 6-8

225 g (8 oz) butter, softened
2 onions, skinned and sliced
450 g (1 lb) turkey or chicken livers
2 × 5 ml tsp prepared mustard
1 × 15 ml tbs lemon juice
finely grated rind of 1 lemon
2 × 15 ml tbs double cream
1 × 5 ml tsp grated nutmeg
2 × 15 ml tbs brandy
175 g (6 oz) ground almonds
salt and pepper

1 Melt 50 g (2 oz) of the butter in a frying pan and fry the onion gently for 5 minutes until soft. Add the livers to the pan and cook gently for a further 5 minutes.

2 Purée the contents of the pan in a blender or food processor. Leave the mixture for 10 minutes to cool slightly.

3 Beat in another 50 g (2 oz) butter and the rest of the ingredients. Season well with salt and pepper and then spoon the mixture into six or eight individual ramekin dishes or a terrine.

4 Melt the remaining butter and pour over the top of the pâté. Chill overnight before serving the pâté.

TOP LEFT Salmon Rillettes
RIGHT Lemon and Almond Liver Pâté

MOUSSELINE OF SOLE WITH PRAWNS

SERVES 6

450 g (1 lb) sole fillets, skinned and chopped
50 g (2 oz) peeled prawns
1 egg white, beaten
¼ × 5 ml tsp salt
¼ × 5 ml tsp ground white pepper
300 ml (10 fl oz) double cream
SAUCE
1 × 5 ml tsp cornflour
2 × 5 ml tsp lemon juice
1 × 5 ml tsp tomato purée
150 ml (5 fl oz) double cream, whipped
peeled prawns, to garnish

Mousseline of Sole with Prawns

1 Combine the chopped fish with the prawns and egg white and season with salt and pepper. Purée the mixture in a blender with the cream.

2 Oil six 150 ml (5 fl oz) ovenproof ramekins and press the mixture well down into the dishes. Cover each dish with a round of foil pleated in the centre; chill for 3 hours.

3 Place the ramekins in a large roasting tin and half fill the tin with boiling water. Bake in the oven at 150°C/300°F/Gas Mark 2 for 30-40 minutes. Stand the ramekins on a wire rack to drain and then keep the mousselines warm.

4 To make the sauce, whisk the cornflour, lemon juice and tomato purée into the cream. Cook over a low heat for 2-3 minutes until thickened, stirring all the time. Remove from the heat, season with salt and pepper to taste.

5 Turn the mousselines out of the ramekins on to serving plates, add the sauce and garnish with prawns.

SEAFOOD PARISIENNE

SERVES 4

227 g pack ready-prepared seafood cocktail
75 ml (3 fl oz) white wine
150 ml (5 fl oz) water
2-3 parsley stalks
1 bay leaf
6 peppercorns
40 g (1½ oz) butter
1 shallot, skinned and finely chopped
115 g (4 oz) button mushrooms, wiped and halved
2 × 15 ml tbs plain flour
75 ml (3 fl oz) milk
2 × 15 ml tbs single cream
salt and pepper
2 × 15 ml tbs fresh breadcrumbs
bay leaves, to garnish

1 Place the seafood in a saucepan with the wine, water, parsley stalks, bay leaf and peppercorns. Simmer very gently for 2-3 minutes, then lift out the seafood with a slotted spoon and set aside. Discard the bay leaf and peppercorns. Remove the parsley stalks and reserve. Reserve the cooking liquid.

2 Melt 25 g (1 oz) of the butter in a saucepan, add the shallot and mushrooms and cook for 3-5 minutes until softened. Add the flour and cook gently for 1 minute, stirring. Gradually stir in the cooking liquid, bring to the boil and cook, stirring constantly, until thickened. Stir in the milk and boil until reduced slightly.

3 Chop the reserved parsley stalks and stir into the sauce with the cream and seafood. Season to taste and spoon into small gratin dishes or scrubbed, deep scallop shells, if wished. Scatter over the breadcrumbs, dot with the remaining butter and grill until browned and bubbling. Serve at once, garnished with bay leaves.

Seafood Parisienne

ASPARAGUS BARQUETTES

MAKES 20–24

225 g (8 oz) plain flour
pinch of salt
175 g (6 oz) butter, diced
3 × 15 ml tbs cold water
FILLING
335 g (12 oz) thin asparagus spears
115 g (4 oz) full-fat soft cheese
2 × 15 ml tbs ready-made pesto sauce
½ sachet aspic jelly powder, dissolved in 300 ml (10 fl oz) boiling water
salt and pepper

1 Sift together the flour and salt and rub in the butter until the mixture resembles fine bread-crumbs. Stir in enough of the water to make a firm elastic dough, then knead lightly on a floured board. Wrap and chill for 15 minutes.

2 Roll out the pastry thinly. Arrange 20-24 barquette (boat-shaped) tins on the work sur-face and lay the pastry on top. Press down the pastry into the tins, then roll the rolling pin over the top to trim.

3 Prick the pastry cases with a fork, then stack the lined tins one on top of another, 4 tins to a stack, on a baking tray and place one spare bar-quette tin on top to prevent the top ones rising. Bake in the oven at 220°C/425°F/Gas Mark 7 for 15 minutes. Remove the spare tins, spread out the lined tins and bake for 5 minutes more. Slide the pastry cases out of the tins and cool.

4 While the pastry cases are cooking, lay the asparagus spears in a frying pan and cover with salted water. Bring to the boil and simmer for 5-8 minutes until tender. Drain and leave to cool, then cut off the asparagus tips and reserve.

5 Blend the asparagus stems in a food proces-sor until smooth, then transfer to a bowl. Beat in the soft cheese, pesto, 3 × 15 ml tbs of the aspic jelly and salt and pepper to taste. Chill until beginning to thicken.

6 Divide the asparagus filling among the pas-try cases and garnish with asparagus tips. Spoon a little aspic jelly over each and chill until set.

CRAB BOUCHEES

MAKES 24

213 g pack chilled ready-made puff pastry
1 egg yolk, beaten with a pinch of salt, to glaze
FILLING
15 g (½ oz) butter
1 shallot, skinned and finely chopped
2 celery sticks, trimmed and finely chopped
1 × 15 ml tbs plain flour
115 ml (4 fl oz) single cream
170 g can white crabmeat, drained
2 × 15 ml tbs mayonnaise
squeeze of lemon juice
2 × 15 ml tbs mild chilli relish
salt and pepper
fresh chives, to garnish

1 Roll out the pastry to a 0.6 cm (¼ in) thick-ness and cut out 12 × 5 cm (2 in) squares. Cut the squares across into triangles and brush the tops with the beaten egg. Mark the tops with a criss-cross pattern. Chill for 15 minutes. Arrange on dampened baking trays and bake in the oven at 200°C/400°F/Gas Mark 6 for 10-15 minutes until risen and brown. Cool.

2 Meanwhile, melt the butter in a small pan, add the shallot and celery and cook for 3 min-utes. Add the flour and cook for 1 minute. Stir in the cream and cook until thickened, stirring all the time. Stir in the remaining ingredients. Leave to cool.

3 Split the bouchées in half and fill with the crab mixture. Garnish with chives and serve.

Asparagus Barquettes

CHICKEN LIVER SALAD

SERVES 4

225 g (8 oz) frozen chicken livers, thawed

25 g (1 oz) butter

1 garlic clove, skinned and crushed

1 × 5 ml tsp wholegrain mustard

1 × 5 ml tsp tomato purée

2 × 15 ml tbs balsamic vinegar

3 × 15 ml tbs olive oil

salt and pepper

1-2 × 115 g (4 oz) bags French-style salad leaves

1 Wash the chicken livers and pat dry on absorbent kitchen paper, then cut each into two or three pieces, removing any bitter green patches. Melt the butter in a frying pan, add the livers and garlic and cook over a medium-high heat for about 3 minutes until browned on the outside.

2 Meanwhile, place the mustard, tomato purée, vinegar and olive oil in a small bowl, add salt and pepper to taste and whisk thoroughly. Arrange the salad leaves on individual plates.

3 When the livers are cooked, add the dressing to the pan, swirl round once or twice, then spoon over the lettuce leaves and serve at once.

COOK'S TIP

Bags of ready-prepared salad leaves are now widely available and come in a selection of interesting leafy combinations including some of the following: curly endive or frisé, rocket, watercress, tender young spinach leaves, corn salad (maché or lamb's lettuce), radicchio and crisp lettuce, such as iceberg or Romaine (Cos).

MARINATED VEGETABLES

SERVES 4

4 baby leeks, trimmed and halved lengthways

2 heads chicory, trimmed and halved lengthways

4 baby carrots, trimmed and halved lengthways

6 × 15 ml tbs water

2 garlic cloves, skinned and crushed

6 × 15 ml tbs olive oil

2 × 15 ml tbs white wine vinegar

2 × 15 ml tbs fine orange rind shreds

2 × 15 ml tbs chopped fresh flat-leaf parsley

salt and pepper

1 Place the leeks, chicory and carrots in a saucepan, add the water and cook over a low heat for 12-15 minutes until just tender.

2 Meanwhile, mix together the garlic, oil, vinegar, orange rind, parsley and salt and pepper to taste. When the vegetables are ready, drain thoroughly and place in a serving dish. Pour over the dressing and leave to cool. Place in the refrigerator and leave to marinate for 2 hours before serving.

TOP Marinated Vegetables
BOTTOM Chicken Liver Salad

CHEESE AND
EGG DISHES

The mere thought of egg and cheese dishes and all manner of delectable dishes spring to mind – light, golden omelettes, sensational high-rise soufflés and delicious tarts to mention a few. Some make ideal snacks and supper dishes, whilst others are quite special enough to grace a dinner party table. Soufflés, remember, are not difficult to make, but once cooked must be served immediately, so ensure your guests are ready and waiting ... not the other way round!

OPPOSITE
TOP Spinach and Gruyère Soufflé
BOTTOM Roquefort Feuillete

OMELETTE

SERVES 1

2-3 eggs
salt and pepper
1 × 15 ml tbs milk or water
margarine or butter, for frying

1 Whisk the eggs just enough to break them down – do not make them frothy as overbeating spoils the texture of the omelette. Season with salt and pepper and add the milk or water.
2 Place an omelette or non-stick frying pan over a gentle heat and, when it is hot, add a generous knob of margarine or butter. Heat it until it is foaming but not brown.
3 Add the beaten eggs. Stir gently with a fork or wooden spatula, drawing the mixture from the sides to the centre as it sets and letting the liquid egg in the centre run to the sides. When the eggs have set, stop stirring and cook for another minute until the omelette is golden brown underneath and still creamy on top. Do not overcook or it will be tough.
4 If making a filled omelette, add the filling at this point. Tilt the pan away from you slightly and use a palette knife to fold over a third of the omelette to the centre, then fold over the opposite third. Slide the omelette out on to a warmed plate, letting it flip over so that the folded sides are underneath. Serve at once.

COOK'S TIP

For the classic fines herbes omelette, add 1 × 15 ml tbs finely chopped fresh chervil, chives and tarragon or a large pinch of mixed dried herbs to the beaten egg mixture before cooking.

For cheese omelette, grate 40 g (1½ oz) cheese. Put half of it in the centre of the omelette before folding it. Sprinkle the rest over the finished omelette.

For tomato omelette, fry 1–2 skinned and chopped tomatoes in a little butter until soft. Put in the centre of omelette before folding.

SPINACH AND GRUYERE SOUFFLE

SERVES 3-4

450 g (1 lb) fresh spinach, cooked or 225 g (8 oz) frozen leaf spinach, thawed
50 g (2 oz) margarine or butter
3 × 15 ml tbs plain flour
200 ml (7 fl oz) milk
salt and pepper
3 eggs, separated, plus 1 extra egg white
115 g (4 oz) Gruyère or Emmenthal cheese, grated

1 Grease a 1.3 lt (2¼ pt) soufflé dish. Put the spinach in a sieve and press it to remove all moisture. Finely chop the spinach.
2 Melt the margarine or butter in a saucepan, add the spinach and cook for a few minutes to drive off any remaining liquid.
3 Add the flour and cook gently for 1 minute, stirring. Remove the pan from the heat and gradually stir in the milk. Season with salt and pepper and bring to the boil slowly. Reduce the heat and continue to cook, stirring, until thickened. Cool slightly, then beat in the egg yolks, one at a time, and 75 g (3 oz) of the grated cheese.
4 Whisk all four egg whites together until stiff, then fold into the mixture. Spoon the mixture into the prepared soufflé dish and sprinkle with the remaining cheese.
5 Stand the dish on a baking tray and bake in the oven at 190°C/375°F/Gas Mark 5 for about 30 minutes, or until well risen and just set. Serve immediately.

TOP Omelette Fines Herbes
BOTTOM Omelette

TARTE PROVENCALE

SERVES 6–8

2 × 15 ml tbs Dijon mustard
275 g (10 oz) aubergines, very thinly sliced
1 green pepper, seeded and cut into very fine slices
olive oil, for brushing
3 egg yolks
350 ml (12 fl oz) double cream
1 small garlic clove, skinned and crushed
175 g (6 oz) mature Cheddar cheese, grated
salt and pepper
2 large tomatoes, seeded and thickly sliced
a few black olives
a few chopped fresh herbs, such as marjoram and basil
PASTRY
225 g (8 oz) plain white flour
pinch of salt
pinch of paprika
115 g (4 oz) butter, diced
50 g (2 oz) Gruyère cheese, grated
3-4 × 15 ml tbs water

1 To make the pastry, put the flour, salt and paprika in a bowl. Rub in the fat until the mixture resembles fine breadcrumbs, then stir in the cheese. Mix in enough water to make a stiff dough.
2 Roll out the pastry and use to line a greased 28 cm (11 in) flan tin. Spread the mustard over pastry and chill while preparing the filling.
3 Spread the aubergines in a single layer on an oiled baking tray. Sprinkle over the pepper slices and brush with a little olive oil. Bake at 200°C/400°F/Gas Mark 6 for 20 minutes.
4 Beat together the egg yolks, cream, garlic and cheese, and season with salt and pepper.
5 Arrange the tomato slices in a single layer in the pastry case. Top with the aubergine and pepper slices and sprinkle with the olives. Carefully pour the custard mixture over the vegetables so that it just comes to the top of the pastry.

6 Place on a baking tray and bake at 200°C/400°F/Gas Mark 6 for 30 minutes. Sprinkle with the herbs, then cook for 15-20 minutes until set. Serve warm or cold.

ROQUEFORT FEUILLETE

SERVES 6

225 g (8 oz) onion, skinned and sliced
25 g (1 oz) butter
4 × 15 ml tbs single cream
1 × 15 ml tbs chopped fresh rosemary
black pepper
175 g (6 oz) Roquefort cheese, crumbled
213 g packet chilled puff pastry
1 egg, beaten
sprigs of rosemary, to garnish

1 Cook the onion in the butter until it softens. Drain on absorbent kitchen paper and cool.
2 Whisk together the cream, rosemary and pepper to taste and add the cheese.
3 Divide the pastry in half and roll out each piece thinly to an oblong about 30 × 20 cm (12 × 8 in). Place one on a baking tray.
4 Spread the onion down the centre, leaving a clear border. Spoon over the cheese mixture. Brush the edges with beaten egg, then top with the second piece of pastry, sealing well. Trim and knock up the edges. Glaze with beaten egg and use the pastry trimmings to make decorations for the top. Make a few holes in the top.
5 Bake at 220°C/425°F/Gas Mark 7 for 15 minutes, or until well browned. Turn the oven down to 180°C/350°F/Gas Mark 4. Cover with foil and bake for a further 10 minutes.
6 Cool slightly, cut into slices and serve, garnished with sprigs of rosemary.

Tarte Provençale

Baked Eggs with Broad Beans and Tomato

BAKED EGGS WITH BROAD BEANS AND TOMATO

SERVES 4

335 g (12 oz) frozen broad beans

15 g (½ oz) butter

1 small onion, skinned and finely sliced

2 × 15 ml tbs chopped fresh parsley

3 tomatoes, skinned, seeded and cut into thin shreds

salt and pepper

4 eggs

2 × 15 ml tbs single cream

25 g (1 oz) Gruyère cheese, grated

1 Cook the broad beans in boiling salted water for 5-8 minutes until tender, then drain. Melt the butter in a pan, add the onion and cook over a low heat for 5 minutes until softened. Add the beans, parsley, tomatoes and salt and pepper to taste and cook for 1-2 minutes.

2 Divide the bean mixture among 4 small gratin dishes. Break one egg on top of each, spoon the cream over the yolks and scatter the cheese on top. Bake in the oven at 180°C/350°F/Gas Mark 4 for 15-20 minutes until the eggs are set. Serve at once.

DEEP-FRIED CAMEMBERT WITH RHUBARB SAUCE

SERVES 4

8 Camembert cheese portions
1 × size 1 egg, beaten
115 g (4 oz) fine fresh breadcrumbs
sunflower oil, for deep-frying
green salad leaves, to garnish
SAUCE
225 g (8 oz) rhubarb, trimmed and cut into pieces
40 g (1½ oz) sugar
1 × 15 ml tbs water
¼ × 5 ml tsp ground ginger
salt and pepper

1 To make the sauce, place the rhubarb and sugar in a saucepan with the water. Cover the pan and cook over a low heat for 10 minutes until the rhubarb is very soft.

2 Remove the pan from the heat and blend the rhubarb and liquid in a food processor until smooth. Stir in the ginger and add salt and pepper to taste, then return to the pan and heat through gently.

3 Meanwhile, trim off the rind from the Camembert portions. Beat the egg with salt and pepper to taste and pour on to a large plate. Spread out the breadcrumbs on another plate. Dip the Camembert portions first in egg, then in breadcrumbs. Repeat the process, dipping them carefully a second time.

4 Heat the oil in a deep-fat fryer to 190°C/375°F. Fry the Camembert portions, four at a time, for about 2 minutes until crisp and golden. Drain on absorbent kitchen paper and serve at once with the sauce. Garnish with salad leaves.

Deep-fried Camembert with Rhubarb Sauce

CHEESY CHOUX BUNS

SERVES 4

90 g (3½ oz) plain flour

½ × 5 ml tsp mustard powder

pinch of cayenne pepper

large pinch of salt

75 g (3 oz) butter

215 ml (7½ fl oz) water

3 eggs, beaten

50 g (2 oz) Gruyère cheese, finely grated

sprigs of flat-leaf parsley, to garnish

FILLING

150 g soft cheese with garlic, parsley and pepper

115 g (4 oz) full-fat soft cheese

115 g (4 oz) ham, finely diced

25 g (1 oz) walnuts, chopped

2 × 15 ml tbs chopped parsley

salt and pepper

1 Sift together the flour, mustard powder, cayenne pepper and a large pinch of salt. Place the butter in a pan with the water and heat slowly to melt, then bring to the boil. Add the seasoned flour all at once, and beat well to make a smooth paste that leaves the sides of the pan clean.

2 Allow the paste to cool slightly, before gradually beating in enough of the eggs to give a soft dropping consistency. Beat the cheese into the choux paste.

3 Place 20 equal amounts of the mixture on a dampened baking tray and bake in the oven at 200°C/400°F/Gas Mark 6 for 25-30 minutes until well risen and crisp. Leave the buns to cool on a wire rack.

4 Meanwhile, mix together the soft cheeses, ham, walnuts, parsley and salt and pepper to taste. Split the buns once they are cold and fill with the cheese mixture. Serve at once, garnished with sprigs of flat-leaf parsley.

PIPERADE

SERVES 4

3 × 15 ml tbs olive oil

2 red and 1 green pepper, seeded and cut into 1 cm (½ in) cubes

1 garlic clove, skinned and crushed

5 ripe tomatoes, skinned, seeded and chopped

pinch of chilli powder

6 eggs

4 × 15 ml tbs water

salt and pepper

1 × 15 ml tbs chopped fresh thyme

1 × 15 ml tbs chopped fresh parsley

sprigs of fresh thyme, to garnish

1 Heat the oil in a heavy-based frying pan, add the peppers and garlic and fry for 8-10 minutes until beginning to soften. Stir in the tomatoes and chilli powder and cook for 1-2 minutes more.

2 Beat the eggs with the water, and salt and pepper to taste, then stir into the vegetables. Cook over a low heat for 4-5 minutes, stirring gently, until set. Scatter the herbs over and serve at once, garnished with sprigs of fresh thyme.

COOK'S TIP

This delicious open-style omelette is colourful and rich with the flavour of peppers, garlic and tomatoes. Serve it hot on its own or with a leafy salad or jacket potatoes. Pipérade, served cold, also makes an unusually good filling for crisp baguettes or soft, floury baps.

TOP Cheesy Choux Buns
BOTTOM Pipérade

MEAT AND
POULTRY DISHES

The French are renowned for their stylish cooking, so why not follow their example with these splendid main-course dishes? Show off your culinary skills with a Boeuf en Croûte, or enjoy the simplicity of a classic Coq au Vin. Savour the succulence of duck breasts tangy with raspberries for an anniversary supper – and why not impress the family this Christmas with a turkey cooked in the French style?

OPPOSITE
TOP Boeuf Bourguignon
BOTTOM Raspberry Duck

CARBONNADE OF BEEF

SERVES 4

salt and pepper

900 g (2 lb) stewing steak, cut into 5 cm (2 in) cubes

50 g (2 oz) beef dripping or butter

75 g (3 oz) lean bacon, rinded and chopped

4 × 15 ml tbs plain flour

300 ml (10 fl oz) beer, plus a little extra, if necessary

300 ml (10 fl oz) beef stock

2-3 × 15 ml tbs vinegar

2 × 5 ml tsp soft brown sugar

pinch of grated nutmeg

450 g (1 lb) onions, skinned and chopped

1 garlic clove, skinned and chopped

1 bouquet garni

4 × 1 cm (½ in) slices of French bread

1 × 15 ml tbs French mustard

parsley, to garnish

1 Season the steak. Heat the fat in a frying pan and fry the meat for about 5 minutes until browned. Add the bacon and fry for 3 minutes. Remove the steak and bacon from the pan and set aside.

2 Stir the flour into the pan and brown lightly. Gradually add the beer, stock, vinegar, sugar and nutmeg, stirring continuously until the mixture thickens.

3 Layer the steak, bacon, onions and garlic in a casserole. Pour the sauce over and add the bouquet garni.

4 Cover and cook the casserole in the oven at 150°C/300°F/Gas Mark 2 for 2-2½ hours until the meat is tender. Add a little more beer while cooking, if necessary.

5 Remove the bouquet garni and skim off the fat. Spread the French bread with the mustard and place on top of the stew, pushing the slices into the liquid. Return the casserole, uncovered, to the oven for a further 30 minutes until well browned. Garnish with parsley and serve hot.

STEAK AU POIVRE

SERVES 8

8 sirloin, rump or fillet steaks, trimmed of excess fat

4 × 15 ml tbs black or green peppercorns, coarsely crushed

50 g (2 oz) butter or margarine

2 × 15 ml tbs vegetable oil

salt

4 × 15 ml tbs brandy

300 ml (10 fl oz) double cream

sprigs of flat-leaf parsley, to garnish

1 Place the steaks on the crushed peppercorns and press hard to encrust the surface of the meat. Turn the steaks to encrust the other side of each one.

2 Heat the butter or margarine and oil in a frying pan and fry the steaks for 2 minutes on each side. Reduce the heat and continue cooking the steaks until they are cooked to taste. Season to taste with salt.

3 Remove the steaks from the pan and keep warm. Add the brandy to the pan, remove from the heat and carefully set it alight. Keep off the heat until the flames have died down, then stir in the cream. Season with salt and gently reheat the sauce. Pour sauce around the steaks, garnish with sprigs of flat-leaf parsley and serve.

COOK'S TIP

Green peppercorns have a fresh spicy flavour and are milder than black peppercorns. These little green berries are picked before they are ripe and are dried or bottled in brine.

TOP Steak au Poivre
BOTTOM Carbonnade of Beef

BOEUF EN CROUTE

SERVES 8

1.8 kg (4 lb) beef fillet, in one piece, trimmed

4 × 5 ml tsp brandy

salt and pepper

115 g (4 oz) butter

2 onions, skinned and finely chopped

335 g (12 oz) mushrooms, wiped and finely chopped

2 × 213 g packets chilled puff pastry

175 g (6 oz) smooth pâté (chicken, duck or goose liver)

1 egg, lightly beaten

sprigs of flat-leaf parsley, to garnish

SAUCE

50 g (2 oz) butter

1 small onion, skinned and finely chopped

115 g (4 oz) mushrooms, wiped and finely chopped

2 × 15 ml tbs plain flour

600 ml (20 fl oz) beef stock

300 ml (10 fl oz) red wine

1 Brush the beef with the brandy and season with pepper. Melt the butter in a frying pan, and fry the beef for 2 minutes, turning to seal all over. Remove from the pan and roast at 200°C/400°F/Gas Mark 6 for 15 minutes.

2 Add the onion to the pan and fry for 10 minutes. Add the mushrooms and fry for 4-5 minutes or until most of the moisture has evaporated. Season with salt and pepper and cool. Remove the meat from the oven and cool completely.

3 Roll out the pastry to a large rectangle. Mix the pâté with 4 × 15 ml tbs of the mushroom mixture and spread it over the top of the beef. Place the meat, pâté side down, in the centre of the pastry and cover the meat with the remaining mushroom mixture. Brush the edges of the pastry with beaten egg and wrap the fillet in the pastry. Press the edges to seal and place, join-side down, on a baking tray.

4 Re-roll the pastry trimmings and use them to decorate the pastry. Brush the pastry with beaten egg. Bake at 200°C/400°F/Gas Mark 6 for 20 minutes, or until the pastry is golden brown.

5 Meanwhile, make the sauce. Melt the butter in a saucepan and fry the onion for 5 minutes. Add the mushrooms and cook for a further 3 minutes. Stir in the flour and cook for 1 minute. Gradually stir in the stock and red wine. Bring to the boil and simmer for 10 minutes. Season, strain and serve with the beef. Garnish with sprigs of flat-leaf parsley.

BOEUF BOURGUIGNON

SERVES 8

50 g (2 oz) butter

4 × 15 ml tbs vegetable oil

225 g (8 oz) bacon in a piece, rinded and diced

1.8 kg (4 lb) braising steak or topside, cubed

2 garlic cloves, skinned and crushed

4 × 15 ml tbs plain flour

salt and pepper

1 bouquet garni

300 ml (10 fl oz) beef stock

600 ml (1 pt) red Burgundy

24 small onions, skinned

335 g (12 oz) button mushrooms, wiped

1 Heat half the butter and half the oil in a flame-proof casserole and fry the bacon for 5 minutes. Drain. Fry the steak for about 8 minutes.

2 Return the bacon to the casserole and add the garlic, flour and season with salt and pepper. Add the bouquet garni, stock and wine then bring to the boil, stirring. Cover and cook at 160°C/325°F/Gas Mark 3 for 1½ hours.

3 Meanwhile, heat the remaining butter and oil in a frying pan and fry the whole onions for 10 minutes. Remove from pan. Add the mushrooms to the pan and fry for 5 minutes.

4 Add the mushrooms and onions to the casserole and cook for 30 minutes, or until the meat is tender. Skim before serving.

DAUBE DE BOEUF

SERVES 6

1.1 kg (2½ lb) rolled top rump of beef

50 g (2 oz) stuffed green olives, sliced

salt and pepper

300 ml (10 fl oz) red wine

2 × 15 ml tbs olive oil

2 × 15 ml tbs beef dripping or lard

75 ml (3 fl oz) brandy

1 large onion, skinned and sliced

3 carrots, peeled and sliced

4 tomatoes, skinned and roughly chopped

6 rashers of smoked streaky bacon, rinded

2 garlic cloves, skinned and halved

1 bouquet garni

water, for mixing

1 Make several deep incisions in the beef and insert the slices of olive. Put the beef in a bowl and sprinkle with salt and pepper. Mix together the wine and olive oil and pour over the beef. Cover and marinate for 4-6 hours.

2 Remove the beef from the marinade and pat dry. Reserve the marinade. Melt the dripping in a large flameproof casserole, add the beef and brown quickly on all sides.

3 Heat the brandy gently in a separate small pan or a ladle. Turn off the heat under the casserole, pour in the brandy and set it alight. When the flames have died down, remove the beef from the casserole and set it aside.

4 Add onion and carrots to casserole and fry for 5 minutes. Add tomatoes, then remove vegetables with a slotted spoon. Put the bacon in the casserole and cover with vegetables. Bury the garlic and bouquet garni in the vegetables, top with the beef and add reserved marinade mixed with enough water to come halfway up the meat. Add salt and pepper to taste and bring slowly to boiling point.

5 Cover with foil, then the lid. Cook at 150°C/300°F/Gas Mark 2 for 2½ hours or until the beef is tender.

6 Skim and remove the bouquet garni.

LAMB CASSEROLE

SERVES 4

2 × 15 ml tbs vegetable oil

1 kg (2¼ lb) best end of lamb, divided into cutlets

1 × 5 ml tsp sugar, plus a little extra

1 × 15 ml tbs plain flour

900 ml (1½ pt) chicken stock

2 × 15 ml tbs tomato purée

salt and pepper

1 bouquet garni

225 g (8 oz) button onions, skinned

4 carrots, peeled and sliced

1-2 turnips, peeled and quartered

8 small even-sized potatoes, peeled

225 g (8 oz) fresh peas, shelled,

or 115 g (4 oz) frozen peas

chopped fresh parsley, to garnish

1 Heat the oil in a saucepan and fry the cutlets for about 5 minutes on both sides until lightly browned. If there is too much fat at this stage, pour off a little to leave 1-2 × 15 ml tbs.

2 Stir in 1 × 5 ml tsp of the sugar and heat until it browns slightly. Add the flour, stirring all the time until cooked and browned.

3 Remove the pan from the heat, gradually stir in the stock and bring to the boil. Add the tomato purée, season with salt and pepper then add a pinch more sugar and the bouquet garni. Cover and simmer for about 1 hour.

4 Remove the bouquet garni, add the onions, carrots and turnips and continue cooking for 30 minutes. Add the potatoes and cook for 10 minutes more.

5 Stir in the peas and cook for a further 10 minutes, or until meat and potatoes are tender.

6 Place the meat on a serving dish with the vegetables. Garnish with parsley.

LEFT Daube de Boeuf
RIGHT Lamb Casserole

MARINATED LEG OF LAMB

SERVES 4-6

1.8 kg (4 lb) leg of lamb
2 garlic cloves, skinned and cut into slivers
few rosemary sprigs
salt and pepper
6 × 15 ml tbs olive oil
2 × 15 ml tbs lemon juice
2 × 15 ml tbs white wine vinegar
150 ml (5 fl oz) dry white wine or water
extra rosemary sprigs, to garnish

1 Make deep incisions in the lamb with a sharp, pointed knife. Insert the slivers of garlic and the sprigs of rosemary into the incisions.
2 Rub the outside of the joint all over with plenty of salt and pepper.
3 Mix together the oil, lemon juice and wine vinegar, then brush all over the joint. Place the joint in a flameproof casserole and leave to marinate in the refrigerator for 24 hours.
4 Put the casserole on top of the cooker and fry the joint over moderate heat until browned on all sides. Pour in the wine or water, bring slowly to boiling point then cover and simmer gently for 2 hours or until the lamb is cooked, basting occasionally. Serve hot, garnished with fresh rosemary sprigs.

PORK CHASSEUR

SERVES 4

2 × 15 ml tbs olive oil
675 g (1½ lb) pork fillet, cut into 1 cm (½ in) thick slices
25 g (1 oz) butter
2 shallots or 1 small onion, skinned and finely chopped
175 g (6 oz) button mushrooms, wiped
1 × 15 ml tbs plain flour
115 ml (4 fl oz) dry white wine
2 × 15 ml tbs brandy
1 × 15 ml tbs tomato purée
300 ml (10 fl oz) chicken or veal stock
2 × 15 ml tbs chopped fresh sage
salt and pepper
sage sprigs, to garnish

1 Heat the oil in a large frying pan, add the pork slices and fry over a high heat for about 5 minutes, until browned on both sides. Remove the pork from the pan with a slotted spoon and set aside.
2 Add the butter to the pan and fry the shallots for 3 minutes. Add the mushrooms and cook for 2-3 minutes, then stir in the flour. Cook for 1 minute, before stirring in the white wine, brandy, tomato purée and stock. Bring to the boil.
3 Return the pork to the pan with the sage and salt and pepper to taste. Cover and simmer for 15-20 minutes until the pork is cooked. Transfer to a warmed serving dish and serve garnished with sage sprigs.

TOP Marinated Leg of Lamb
BOTTOM Pork Chasseur

CASSOULET

SERVES 8

450 g (1 lb) dried haricot beans
3 × 15 ml tbs olive oil
450 g (1 lb) coarse pork sausages
225 g (8 oz) smoked bacon in one piece, cut into bite-sized chunks
4 duckling leg portions about 335 g (12 oz) each, skinned, trimmed of excess fat and each split in two
450 g (1 lb) onions, skinned and sliced
450 g (1 lb) tomatoes, peeled and roughly chopped
150 ml (5 fl oz) white wine
2 × 15 ml tbs tomato purée
2 garlic cloves, skinned and crushed
salt and pepper
a bunch of fresh herbs, such as thyme and marjoram, tied together
roughly chopped fresh flat-leaf parsley, to garnish

1 Soak the beans overnight in cold water. The next day, drain, and rinse well with fresh water. Cover with fresh cold water and boil rapidly for 10 minutes, then simmer for about 1 hour, or until the beans are just tender. Drain the beans, reserving 300 ml (10 fl oz) of the cooking liquid and set aside.

2 Heat the oil in a large flameproof casserole. Add the sausages and bacon and lightly brown. Remove from the casserole and drain on absorbent kitchen paper. Coarsely slice the sausages and set aside with the bacon. Add the duckling to the casserole and lightly brown. Drain on absorbent kitchen paper and set aside.

3 Stir the onions into the casserole and cook until they begin to colour. Mix in the beans, tomatoes, the duckling, the sausage and bacon. Add the wine with the reserved cooking liquid, the tomato purée and garlic and season with salt and pepper. Mix well then add the herbs.

4 Bring the liquid to the boil, cover tightly and bake at 160°C/325°F/Gas Mark 3 for 1-1¼ hours, or until all the ingredients are tender and most of the liquid has been absorbed.

5 Uncover the casserole and, if necessary, boil the juices to reduce slightly. Adjust the seasoning, garnish with the parsley and serve warm.

PORC AUX PRUNES

SERVES 4

175 g (6 oz) large ready-to-eat stoned, dried prunes
300 ml (10 fl oz) red wine
2 × 15 ml tbs olive oil
4 boneless pork loin chops, about 150 g (5 oz) each
1 garlic clove, skinned and crushed
1 × 15 ml tbs redcurrant jelly
1 × 15 ml tbs tomato purée
salt and pepper
2 × 15 ml tbs double cream

1 Place the prunes in a bowl with the wine and leave to soak while you cook the pork. Heat the oil in a large frying pan, add the chops and fry over a high heat for 6-8 minutes until browned on both sides.

2 Add the garlic and cook for 30 seconds, then stir in the prunes and wine, redcurrant jelly, tomato purée and salt and pepper to taste. Simmer, uncovered, for 15-20 minutes until the wine is reduced and the chops tender. Stir in the cream and serve hot.

COOK'S TIP

Agen prunes from France are an especially delicious variety – and are splendid cooked this way with pork and wine. For an interesting tangy variation use ready-to-eat (no-need-to-soak) dried apricots or peaches instead of the prunes.

TOP AND BOTTOM Cassoulet
CENTRE Porc aux Prunes

CHICKEN MARENGO

SERVES 4

4 chicken portions
50 g (2 oz) plain flour
115 ml (4 fl oz) olive oil
50 g (2 oz) butter
1 onion, skinned and sliced
2 × 15 ml tbs brandy
salt and pepper
450 g (1 lb) tomatoes, skinned or 2 × 227 g cans tomatoes, with their juice, roughly chopped
1 garlic clove, skinned and crushed
150 ml (5 fl oz) chicken stock
115 g (4 oz) button mushrooms, wiped

1 Coat the chicken portions in the flour. Heat the oil in a large frying pan and fry the chicken on both sides for about 5-10 minutes, until golden brown. Remove the chicken from the frying pan and place, skin-side up, in a large saucepan or flameproof casserole together with 25 g (1 oz) butter.

2 Add the onion to the oil in the frying pan and cook for 5 minutes until soft. Sprinkle the chicken joints with the brandy and salt and pepper and turn the joints over.

3 Add the tomatoes to the chicken with the onion, garlic and stock. Cover and simmer gently for about 1 hour, or until the chicken is cooked.

4 Ten minutes before serving, melt the remaining butter in a pan, add the mushrooms and cook them for about 5 minutes, until soft. Drain the mushrooms and add them to the chicken.

5 When the chicken joints are cooked, transfer them to a warmed serving dish. If the sauce is too thin, boil briskly to reduce. Spoon the sauce over the chicken and serve hot.

COQ AU VIN

SERVES 4

3 × 15 ml tbs olive oil
1.6 kg (3½ lb) roasting chicken (preferably corn-fed), cut into 8 pieces
225 g (8 oz) small button onions, skinned
200 g diced bacon or continental-style lardons
2 garlic cloves, skinned and crushed
1 bouquet garni
salt and pepper
2 × 15 ml tbs brandy
425 ml (15 fl oz) red Burgundy wine
1 × 15 ml tbs tomato purée
25 g (1 oz) butter, softened
25 g (1 oz) plain flour

1 Heat the oil in a large flameproof casserole and brown the chicken for about 5 minutes over a moderate heat. Add the onions and bacon to the pan and cook for 2-3 minutes until browned.

2 Add the garlic, bouquet garni and salt and pepper to taste. Pour the brandy and wine into the pan and stir in the tomato purée. Bring to the boil, reduce the heat, cover the pan and simmer gently for 1 hour, turning the chicken occasionally. If you prefer, the chicken can be transferred to the oven and cooked at 180°C/350°F/Gas Mark 4 for 1½ hours.

3 Remove the bouquet garni. Beat together the butter and flour to make a *beurre manié*. Whisk small knobs of the *beurre manié* into the cooking liquid. Cook until boiling and thickened, then adjust the seasoning if necessary and serve hot.

TOP Chicken Marengo
BOTTOM Coq au Vin

NORMANDY CHICKEN

SERVES 4

2 × 15 ml tbs vegetable oil
40 g (1½ oz) butter
4 chicken portions
6 eating apples
salt and pepper
300 ml (10 fl oz) dry cider
4 × 15 ml tbs Calvados
4 × 15 ml tbs double cream (optional)

1 Heat the oil with 25 g (1 oz) of the butter in a large flameproof casserole. Add the chicken portions and fry over a moderate heat until golden brown on all sides. Remove the chicken from the casserole, drain on absorbent kitchen paper and set aside.

2 Peel, core and slice four of the apples. Add to the casserole and fry gently, tossing constantly, until lightly coloured.

3 Return the chicken portions to the casserole, placing them on top of the apples. Season with salt and pepper to taste, then pour in the cider. Bring to the boil, then cover and cook in the oven at 180°C/350°F/Gas Mark 4 for 45 minutes, or until the chicken portions are cooked.

4 Meanwhile, peel, core and slice the remaining apples. Melt the remaining 15 g (½ oz) butter in a frying pan, add the apple slices and toss to coat in the fat. Fry until lightly coloured, then spoon the apple slices over the chicken.

5 Warm the Calvados gently in a ladle or small pan, then ignite and pour over the chicken and apples. Serve the chicken as soon as the flames have died down, drizzled with cream, if liked.

PATE CHICKEN

SERVES 4

15 g (½ oz) butter
2 × 5 ml tsp vegetable oil
4 chicken portions
1 × 5 ml tsp chopped fresh rosemary or ½ × 5 ml tsp dried rosemary
salt and pepper
4 × 15 ml tbs dry white wine
6 × 15 ml tbs chicken stock
50 g (2 oz) smooth liver pâté
3 × 15 ml tbs single cream
few sautéed sliced button mushrooms, to garnish

1 Heat the butter with the oil in a large frying pan. Add the chicken portions, sprinkle with the rosemary and add salt and pepper to taste. Fry over moderate heat for 15-20 minutes, or until the chicken is well coloured on all sides.

2 Pour in half the wine and half the stock, bring to the boil, then lower the heat, cover the pan and continue cooking for a further 10-15 minutes, or until the chicken is cooked. Remove the chicken from the pan with a slotted spoon.

3 Strip the skin off the chicken portions and discard. Place the chicken on a serving platter, cover and keep hot while making the sauce.

4 Add the remaining wine and stock to the pan and stir to combine with the cooking juices. Boil the liquid vigorously for a few minutes to reduce it slightly.

5 Meanwhile, beat the pâté and cream together until they are smooth and well combined.

6 Gradually whisk the pâté mixture into the wine and stock over low heat. Cook gently for 1-2 minutes, stirring constantly, then taste and adjust the seasoning, if necessary. Pour over the chicken, garnish with a few sautéed mushrooms and serve immediately.

Normandy Chicken

FRENCH ROAST CHESTNUT TURKEY

SERVES 8–10

675 g (1½ lb) chestnuts
425 ml (15 fl oz) chicken stock or water
1 large onion, skinned and roughly chopped
2 celery sticks, trimmed and finely chopped
450 g (1 lb) spicy Continental pork sausage, skinned and finely chopped
50 ml (2 fl oz) brandy
2 × 15 ml tbs chopped mixed fresh herbs
salt and pepper
1 egg, beaten
4 kg (9 lb) oven-ready turkey
50 g (2 oz) butter, melted
sprigs of thyme and flat-leaf parsley, to garnish

1 Nick the skin of chestnuts, plunge into boiling water. Boil for 15 minutes, then drain.

2 Peel the chestnuts, then place in a saucepan with the stock, onion and celery. Simmer for 20 minutes until just tender.

3 Remove the chestnuts from the liquid with a slotted spoon. Reserve half and purée the remainder in a blender or food processor, with a little of the cooking liquid.

4 Put the puréed chestnuts in a bowl with the chopped sausage, brandy, herbs and salt and pepper to taste. Strain the remaining cooking liquid and reserve. Add the onion and celery to the stuffing and mix with the beaten egg.

5 Stuff the neck of the turkey, then truss and put the turkey on a rack in a roasting tin.

6 Brush with butter and sprinkle with salt and pepper. Pour enough of the reserved chestnut cooking liquid into the tin to just cover the base.

7 Roast the turkey at 190°C/375°F/Gas Mark 5 for 3 hours. Add more chestnut liquid to the tin if it becomes dry during roasting, and add the reserved whole chestnuts and the remaining liquid 30 minutes before the end of the cooking time.

8 When cooked, transfer the turkey to a warmed dish and leave to stand for 15-30 minutes in a warm place before carving. Serve the chestnuts around the turkey. Garnish with thyme and parsley and serve the cooking liquid separately.

RASPBERRY DUCK

SERVES 2

2 × 15 ml tbs brandy
juice of 2 limes
2 × 15 ml tbs clear honey
salt and pepper
2 duckling breasts, skinned
15 g (½ oz) butter
2 × 15 ml tbs vegetable oil
225 g (8 oz) fresh or frozen raspberries
300 ml (10 fl oz) rosé wine
blanched shreds of lime zest, to garnish

1 To make the marinade, mix together the brandy, lime juice and half the honey, with salt and pepper to taste.

2 Place the duck breasts in a shallow dish. Pour the marinade over and leave to stand for 4 hours in a cool place turning occasionally.

3 Melt the butter with the oil in a frying pan. Remove the breasts from the marinade and fry over high heat for a few minutes. Turn and fry for a further 5 minutes or until cooked.

4 Meanwhile, put the raspberries in a saucepan with the marinade and wine. Heat gently for 5 minutes, then remove one quarter of the raspberries with a slotted spoon and set aside. Add the remaining honey to the pan and boil until reduced to about half.

5 Strain through a sieve, pressing the raspberries with the back of a spoon. Return to the rinsed-out pan with the reserved whole raspberries and reheat. Taste for sweetness and adjust the seasoning.

6 Slice the duck breasts neatly, then arrange on warmed serving plates with the sauce. Garnish with lime shreds and serve immediately.

French Roast Chestnut Turkey

FISH AND
SHELLFISH DISHES

*It is hardly surprising that fish and shellfish feature so
extensively in French cooking when you think that France has
around 2700 kilometres of coastline to its credit. There is
nothing to match the flavours, variety and versatility of fish –
as the following recipes prove – whether it is a robust fish
stew; the simple succulence of salmon cooked en papillote; or
a stylish Hot Fish Terrine.*

LA BOURRIDE

SERVES 4

6 garlic cloves, skinned
300 ml (10 fl oz) ready-made mayonnaise
finely grated rind of ½ small lemon
900 g (2 lb) white fish fillets, skinned and cut into chunks
1.2 lt (2 pt) fish stock
1 small onion, skinned and thinly sliced
1 leek, trimmed and thinly sliced
1-2 parsley sprigs
1 bay leaf
1 thin strip of orange rind
salt and pepper
1 small baguette (French stick), sliced, to serve
chopped fresh parsley and grated orange rind, to garnish

1 Crush 4 garlic cloves and mix into the mayonnaise with the lemon rind.

2 Put the fish into a large saucepan. Pour in the stock, then add the next five ingredients, and 2 garlic cloves, halved. Season with salt and pepper to taste. Cover and simmer for 15 minutes, until tender.

3 With a slotted spoon, transfer the fish and vegetables to a warmed serving dish. Keep warm. Strain the cooking liquid into a jug and blend a few spoonfuls into the mayonnaise. Toast the sliced baguette and keep warm.

4 Put the mayonnaise in a heavy-based pan, then gradually whisk in the remaining cooking liquid. Heat through gently, stirring constantly. Adjust the seasoning. Pour over the fish and sprinkle parsley and orange rind over the top. Serve at once, with the toasted baguette slices.

HOT FISH TERRINE

SERVES 6

90 g (2½ oz) butter
1 garlic clove, skinned and crushed
4 × 15 ml tbs plain flour
750 ml (1¼ pt) milk
565 g (1¼ lb) hake fillets, skinned and chopped
150 ml (5 fl oz) double cream
3 eggs
1 egg yolk
salt and pepper
2 × 15 ml tbs chopped fresh parsley
115 g (4 oz) peeled prawns, chopped
115 g (4 oz) Gruyère cheese, grated
watercress sprigs and 8 peeled prawns, to garnish

1 Lightly grease and base line a 1.6 lt (2¾ pt) shallow loaf tin or terrine. Melt 40 g (1½ oz) butter in a saucepan. Add the garlic, stir in 3 × 15 ml tbs of the flour and cook for 2 minutes. Remove from the heat and stir in 425 ml (15 fl oz) of the milk. Bring to the boil, stirring. Simmer for 2 minutes.

2 In a blender, purée the sauce, fish, cream, eggs and yolk. Season with salt and pepper.

3 Spoon half the mixture into the tin. Sprinkle with parsley and half the prawns. Spoon in the rest of the mixture. Cover tightly with buttered greaseproof paper.

4 Place in a roasting tin with hot water to come halfway up the sides of the tin. Cook at 150°C/300°F/Gas Mark 2 for 1¼ hours.

5 Melt the remaining butter in a pan. Stir in remaining flour and cook for 2 minutes. Remove from the heat and stir in remaining milk. Bring to the boil, stirring. Simmer for 2 minutes. Off the heat, stir in the cheese and remaining prawns. Season with salt and pepper to taste.

6 Invert the terrine on to a warm dish and tilt slightly to drain off any juice. Garnish with watercress and prawns and serve with the sauce.

Hot Fish Terrine

STUFFED SOLE PAUPIETTES

SERVES 6

75 g (3 oz) butter
½ onion, skinned and chopped
225 g (8 oz) button mushrooms, wiped and trimmed
75 g (3 oz) fresh white breadcrumbs
finely grated rind of 1 lemon
1 × 15 ml tbs chopped fresh tarragon leaves
salt and pepper
18 lemon sole quarter-cut fillets (two from each side of the fish), skinned
300 ml (10 fl oz) dry white wine
150 ml (5 fl oz) water
2 × 15 ml tbs plain flour
6 × 15 ml tbs double cream, at room temperature
fresh tarragon sprigs, to garnish

1 To make the stuffing, melt 25 g (1 oz) of the butter in a saucepan. Add the onion and fry gently until lightly coloured.

2 Meanwhile, finely slice half the mushrooms and reserve. Chop the remainder very finely. Put the chopped mushrooms in a bowl with the breadcrumbs, lemon rind and tarragon.

3 Add the softened onion and season with salt and pepper to taste; stir well until combined.

4 Place a sole fillet, skinned-side uppermost, on a board. Put a teaspoonful of stuffing on one end of the fillet. Roll the fish up around it. Secure with a cocktail stick.

5 Stand the fish upright in a well-buttered baking dish. Repeat with remaining sole fillets, placing them side by side in the dish. Mix together the wine and water and pour over the fish. Cover loosely and bake at 190°C/375°F/Gas Mark 5 for 15 minutes.

6 Remove the fish from the cooking liquid with a slotted spoon and discard the cocktail sticks. Place the fish in a single layer in a warmed serving dish, cover and keep warm. Strain the liquid into a jug.

7 Melt 25 g (1 oz) butter in a saucepan, sprinkle in the flour and cook for 1-2 minutes, stirring. Remove from the heat and then gradually stir in the strained cooking liquid. Bring to the boil, reduce the heat and simmer gently for 5 minutes, stirring until thick.

8 Meanwhile, melt the remaining butter in a frying pan, add the finely sliced mushrooms and fry gently. Whisk the cream into the sauce. Pour a little sauce over each paupiette then garnish with the sliced mushrooms and tarragon sprigs. Pour any remaining sauce into a warmed sauceboat and serve separately.

SALMON EN PAPILLOTE

SERVES 4

25 g (1 oz) butter
115 g (4 oz) mange-tout, trimmed and sliced diagonally
4 salmon fillets or steaks, each weighing about 150 g (5 oz) each
1 large orange
2 × 15 ml tbs chopped fresh parsley
1 × 15 ml tbs capers, drained and rinsed
salt and pepper

1 Cut four rounds of greaseproof paper 30 cm (12 in) in diameter. Smear the centres with half the butter, divide the mange-tout among them and top with salmon steaks.

2 Pare one or two thin strips of rind from the orange, cut into thin slivers, then grate the remaining rind over the fish. Scatter the strips of rind over with the parsley, capers and add salt and pepper to taste.

3 Squeeze the juice from the orange over the steaks, dot with remaining butter, then roll and fold the edges of the paper together to enclose completely to seal. Transfer the parcels to a baking tray and bake at 190°C/375°F/Gas Mark 5 for 20-25 minutes. Serve hot.

LEMONY TROUT

SERVES 4

2 × 15 ml tbs plain flour

salt and pepper

4 trout, each weighing about 225 g (8 oz)

50 g (2 oz) butter

2 × 15 ml tbs olive oil

50 g (2 oz) flaked almonds

grated rind of 1 lemon

200 ml (7 fl oz) crème fraîche

sprigs of flat-leaf parsley, to garnish

1 Place the flour and seasoning on a large plate, and dust the trout until well coated. Heat the butter and oil in a large frying pan until foaming, then add the trout and fry over a moderate heat for 8-10 minutes, turning once, until the trout is cooked and the skin crisp and golden. Transfer to a dish and keep warm.

2 Add the almonds and lemon rind to the pan and fry for 2-3 minutes until golden. Stir in the crème fraîche and heat through, stirring all the time. Add seasoning to taste and pour over the trout. Serve at once, garnished with parsley.

Lemony Trout

COD WITH BACON AND SWEET PEPPERS

SERVES 4

4 × 15 ml tbs olive oil

1 red and 1 yellow pepper, seeded and cut into thin strips

2 smoked bacon chops, each weighing about 115 g (4 oz) cut into thin strips

4 skinned cod fillets, each weighing about 115 g (4 oz)

salt and pepper

6 green olives, stoned and cut into thin slivers

1 Heat the oil in a large frying pan and add the peppers and bacon. Fry for 5-8 minutes until the peppers are softened and the bacon cooked. Remove the peppers and bacon from the pan with a slotted spoon and set aside.

2 Add the cod fillets to the pan, season to taste with salt and pepper and cook over a moderate heat for 2-3 minutes until lightly browned underneath. Turn them over, return the peppers and bacon to the pan with the olives and cook for 6-8 minutes more until the fish is cooked through. Serve hot.

COOK'S TIP

Instead of cod fillets, use any white fish such as haddock or whiting for a change, or choose salmon fillets for a special occasion meal.

Cod with Bacon and Sweet Peppers

VEGETABLE

DISHES

*Take a few tips from the French and discover how to fully
appreciate the great variety of fresh vegetables now widely
available to us all. From the exotic artichoke to the humble
parsnip, these recipes show you how vegetables can be
transformed into a wonderful range of dishes, through simple
yet imaginative cooking methods. Here you will find delicious
crisp-topped gratins; delicate little castles of puréed vegetables,
bathed in a creamy cheese sauce; an unusual baked courgette
salad; and a dish of mixed spring vegetables, enhanced with a
lemon glaze – a selection of inspiring ideas, proving that
cooking the French way brings out the best in vegetables.*

OPPOSITE
TOP Onions à la Grecque
BOTTOM Artichoke and Potato Bake

ARTICHOKE AND POTATO BAKE

SERVES 6

150 ml (5 fl oz) single cream
425 ml (15 fl oz) milk
675 g (1½ lb) potatoes, peeled and thinly sliced
400 g can artichoke bottoms, drained and thinly sliced
2 garlic cloves, skinned and crushed
salt and pepper
2 × 15 ml tbs fresh chopped thyme
25 g (1 oz) butter
chopped thyme, to garnish

1 Whisk together the cream and milk. In a shallow flameproof dish layer the potatoes, artichokes and crushed garlic, seasoning between the layers and sprinkling liberally with chopped thyme. Top with a neat potato layer and pour the cream mixture over. Dot with the butter.

2 Stand the dish on a baking tray and bake at 180°C/350°F/Gas Mark 4 for 1½-1¾ hours or until the potatoes are tender and most of the liquid has been absorbed. Garnish with chopped thyme and serve at once.

PARSNIP AND CARROT AU GRATIN

SERVES 4–6

450 g (1 lb) parsnips, peeled and coarsely chopped
450 g (1 lb) carrots, peeled and coarsely chopped
600 ml (20 fl oz) chicken stock
salt and pepper
25 g (1 oz) butter
50 g (2 oz) fresh breadcrumbs
chopped fresh parsley, to garnish

1 Put the parsnips and carrots in a saucepan with the stock and season with salt and pepper to taste. Bring to the boil, cover and simmer the vegetables gently for 15-20 minutes until they are well cooked. Drain and cool slightly.

2 Purée the vegetables in a blender or rub through a sieve. Add the butter and place in a flameproof dish. Sprinkle the breadcrumbs over the surface and cook under a hot grill until the top turns golden brown. Garnish the gratin with parsley and serve hot.

ONIONS A LA GRECQUE

SERVES 8

900 g (2 lb) small pickling onions
5 × 15 ml tbs olive oil
1 × 15 ml tbs clear honey
300 ml (10 fl oz) water
150 ml (5 fl oz) dry white wine
2 × 5 ml tsp tomato purée
salt and pepper
115 g (4 oz) seedless raisins
2 × 15 ml tbs chopped fresh coriander or parsley

1 Blanch the onions in boiling water for 1 minute only, then drain and rinse under cold running water. Remove the onion skins carefully with your fingers and a small, sharp knife.

2 Put the onions in a large, heavy-based saucepan with the olive oil, honey, water, wine and tomato purée. Season with salt and pepper to taste. Bring to the boil, then cover and simmer gently for 30 minutes.

3 Add the raisins to the pan and continue cooking, uncovered, for a further 15 minutes, or until the onions are tender but still whole. Taste and adjust the seasoning if necessary, then stir in the chopped coriander. Serve hot.

Parsnip and Carrot au Gratin

LENTILS COOKED WITH BAY

SERVES 6–8

about 8 whole cloves
1 onion, skinned
225 g (8 oz) green lentils, rinsed in cold water and drained
4 bay leaves
2 celery sticks or 1 carrot (optional)
salt and pepper
1 × 15 ml tbs extra-virgin olive oil
a splash of balsamic or red wine vinegar
bay leaves, to garnish

1 Stick the cloves into the onion. Put this into a large saucepan with the lentils, bay leaves and celery or carrot, if using. Cover with plenty of cold water and bring to the boil. Boil rapidly for 10 minutes. Add plenty of salt. Reduce the heat, cover and simmer gently for 10-20 minutes or until the lentils are tender.

2 Drain the lentils and discard the bay leaves and celery or carrot, if used. Reserve the liquid for making stocks, sauces and gravies. Place the lentils in a serving dish and season with pepper and a little more salt, if necessary. Toss with the olive oil and vinegar. Serve hot or cold, garnished with bay leaves.

Lentils Cooked with Bay

GARLICKY GREEN BEANS WITH TOMATOES

SERVES 4–6

450 g (1 lb) French beans, trimmed and halved

salt and pepper

2 × 15 ml tbs olive oil

2 garlic cloves, skinned and crushed

225 g (8 oz) cherry tomatoes, halved

Garlicky Green Beans with Tomatoes

1 Cook the beans in boiling salted water for 2-3 minutes until just tender, then drain.

2 Heat the oil in the pan, add the garlic and tomatoes and cook for 1-2 minutes until the tomatoes are beginning to soften.

3 Stir in the green beans and season well with pepper. Toss together until hot, then serve at once, or leave to cool and serve cold.

CAULIFLOWER AND BROCCOLI TIMBALES

SERVES 4

225 g (8 oz) cauliflower florets
225 g (8 oz) broccoli florets
salt and pepper
50 g (2 oz) butter
2 eggs, beaten
freshly grated nutmeg
diced tomato, to garnish
SAUCE
15 g (½ oz) butter
1 × 15 ml tbs plain flour
200 ml (7 fl oz) milk
40 g (1½ oz) Gruyère cheese, grated
1 × 5 ml tsp Dijon mustard
1 tomato, skinned, seeded and finely diced
pinch of cayenne pepper

1 Cook the cauliflower and broccoli florets in separate saucepans of boiling salted water for 5-8 minutes until tender. Drain very well, then place the cauliflower in a food processor with 25 g (1 oz) of the butter, half of the egg, nutmeg and plenty of salt and pepper. Blend until smooth.
2 Blend the broccoli separately with the remaining egg and butter and salt and pepper.
3 Butter four 150 ml (5 fl oz) moulds and line the bases with greaseproof paper. Divide the broccoli purée among the moulds, then spoon over the cauliflower purée. Cover each mould with a piece of buttered foil. Place on a baking tray and bake at 180°C/350°F/Gas Mark 4 for 40-45 minutes or until set.
4 About 5 minutes before the end of the cooking time, make the sauce. Melt the butter in a saucepan, add the flour and cook gently over a low heat for 1 minute, stirring. Remove the pan from the heat and gradually stir in the milk, then return the pan to the heat and cook, stir-ring, until boiling and thickened. Stir in the cheese, mustard, tomato and salt and pepper to taste.
5 Turn out the moulds on to plates, spoon around the sauce, dust with cayenne pepper and serve at once, garnished with diced tomato.

LEMON-GLAZED VEGETABLES

SERVES 4

225 g (8 oz) baby carrots, trimmed
225 g (8 oz) turnip, trimmed and cut into lengths
4 celery sticks, trimmed and cut in three crossways on the diagonal
300 ml (10 fl oz) water
grated rind and juice of 1 lemon
sprig of fresh chervil
1½ × 15 ml tbs sugar
25 g (1 oz) butter
salt and pepper
4 small courgettes, trimmed and cut into lengths
2 × 15 ml tbs chopped fresh chervil, to garnish

1 Place the carrots, turnips and celery in a heavy-based saucepan and pour the water over. Add the lemon rind and juice, chervil sprig, sugar, butter and salt and pepper to taste.
2 Lay a buttered paper on top of the vegetables, bring to the boil and simmer for 10 minutes. Add the courgettes and cook, uncovered, for about 5 minutes, turning occasionally, until tender. Using a slotted spoon, remove the vegetables and keep warm. Boil the sauce for 3 minutes until thickened to a lemony glaze, then pour over the vegetables. Garnish with the chervil and serve.

TOP Cauliflower and Broccoli Timbales
BOTTOM Lemon-glazed Vegetables

COS LETTUCE SALAD WITH ANCHOVIES, BACON AND EGGS

SERVES 4

4 eggs
225 g (8 oz) smoked back bacon rashers
2 × 15 ml tbs olive oil
25 g (1 oz) butter
2 thick slices firm-textured wholemeal bread, cubed
1 cos lettuce, washed well
50 g can anchovy fillets, drained and chopped
25 g (1 oz) Gruyère cheese, pared into thin shavings with a potato peeler, to garnish
DRESSING
2 × 15 ml tbs white wine vinegar
6 × 15 ml tbs olive oil
1 × 5 ml tsp Dijon mustard
2 garlic cloves, skinned and crushed
2 × 15 ml tbs finely chopped fresh parsley
salt and pepper

1 Place the eggs in a pan of cold water, bring to the boil, then simmer for 7 minutes. Drain, and cool under cold running water. Meanwhile, grill the bacon until crisp and brown. Heat the oil and butter together in a frying pan and fry the bread cubes until crisp and golden. Drain the bacon and bread cubes on absorbent kitchen paper. Snip the bacon into thin strips.

2 Shell the cooled eggs and cut into wedges. Place the lettuce leaves in a large salad bowl. Scatter the bacon and croûtons over the lettuce, then add the eggs and the anchovies.

3 Make the dressing; whisk together the vinegar, oil, mustard and garlic until well mixed, and stir in the parsley. Season with salt and pepper to taste. Pour over the salad just before serving and toss gently. Scatter over the shavings of Gruyère cheese and serve.

BAKED COURGETTE SALAD

SERVES 4

50 g (2 oz) long-grain rice
4 × 15 ml tbs olive oil
2 shallots, skinned and finely chopped
1 garlic clove, skinned and crushed
4 courgettes, trimmed and halved lengthways
1 small aubergine, trimmed and finely diced
1 red pepper, seeded and diced
4 tomatoes, peeled, seeded and diced
2 × 15 ml tbs chopped walnuts
salt and pepper

1 Cook the rice in boiling salted water for 10-12 minutes until tender, then drain. Heat half of the oil in a small frying pan and cook the shallots and garlic for 3 minutes.

2 Scoop out the middle, seedy part of the courgettes, place the courgette shells in a flameproof dish and set aside. Chop the courgette middles roughly and add to the pan with the aubergine and red pepper and cook, stirring occasionally, for 10 minutes until very tender.

3 Stir in the rice, tomatoes and walnuts, season to taste with salt and pepper and bake at 200°C/400°F/Gas Mark 6 for about 30 minutes until the courgettes are tender and the filling beginning to brown. Drizzle the remaining olive oil over the top, and leave to cool slightly. Serve warm, either on their own or as an accompaniment.

TOP Cos Lettuce Salad with Anchovies, Bacon and Eggs
BOTTOM Baked Courgette Salad

DESSERTS

*French cuisine is hard to beat when it comes to choosing a
dessert that will inspire and delight. In the tempting selection
given on the following pages you will discover timeless classics
such as the luscious hazelnut vacherin, rich with cream and
fruit, or the more rustic Clafouti – an irresistible dish of fresh
cherries baked in a light batter. A gloriously sticky upside-
down apple tart and the simple freshness of pears poached in
wine make memorable finales to any meal.*

TARTE TATIN

SERVES 8

115 g (4 oz) butter, chilled
225 g (8 oz) plain flour
salt
50 g (2 oz) caster sugar
½ × 5 ml tsp vanilla essence
3 × 15 ml tbs crème fraîche or fromage frais
6 × 15 ml tbs chilled water
FILLING
5-6 large dessert apples, about 900 g (2 lb) total weight
lemon juice
75 g (3 oz) unsalted butter, softened
115 g (4 oz) caster sugar

1 To make the pastry, cut the butter into small cubes, about 0.6 cm (¼ in) in size. Mix the flour, salt and sugar together in a bowl, add the butter and stir in the vanilla essence, the crème fraîche and the chilled water. Stir gently. The dough will be very crumbly. Bring together with one hand. Do not knead. Wrap the pastry in cling film for 1 hour.

2 Peel, quarter and core the apples. Toss in a little lemon juice. Spread the softened butter over the base of a 23 cm (9 in) round flameproof dish and sprinkle the sugar evenly over the top. Pack the apples, rounded-sides down, and almost overlapping, into the dish to cover the base completely.

3 Place the dish directly over a moderate heat for about 10 minutes, or until the sugar and butter begin to caramelise. Make sure that the apples do not burn and that the sugar caramelises evenly.

4 Meanwhile, roll out the pastry to the size of the dish and place over the caramelised apples. Stand the dish on a baking tray and bake at 220°C/425°F/Gas Mark 7 for 20 minutes.

5 Put a dish over the tart and carefully invert it. The apples should be sticky and the pastry crisp. Serve hot.

ALMOND PEACH TART

SERVES 6

115 g (4 oz) plain flour
25 g (1 oz) caster sugar
25 g (1 oz) ground almonds
1 × 5 ml tsp grated lemon rind
75 g (3 oz) butter, diced
1 egg yolk
FILLING
4 ripe peaches, peeled, stoned and thinly sliced
2 × 15 ml tbs caster sugar
2 × 15 ml tbs apricot jam
25 g (1 oz) toasted flaked almonds

1 To make the pastry, mix together the flour, sugar, almonds and lemon rind. Add the butter and rub in lightly with the fingertips. Add the egg yolk and mix to a firm dough. Wrap the dough in cling film and chill for 20 minutes.

2 Roll out the dough to a 25 cm (10 in) round and place on a baking tray. Pinch round the edge and prick the base several times. Bake at 190°C/375°F/Gas Mark 5 for 15 minutes.

3 Arrange the peach slices on the pastry base in two rings. Sprinkle evenly with the caster sugar and return the tart to the oven. Bake for 10 minutes longer.

4 Warm the jam and brush evenly over the peaches. Sprinkle with toasted almonds and leave the tart to cool.

Tarte Tatin

STRAWBERRY MILLE FEUILLES

SERVES 6–8

213 g pack chilled ready-made puff pastry
50 g (2 oz) raspberries
2 × 15 ml tbs redcurrant jelly
335 g (12 oz) strawberries, hulled and halved
150 ml (5 fl oz) double cream, whipped
strawberry leaves, to decorate
CREME PATISSIERE
300 ml (10 fl oz) milk
1 vanilla pod, split
3 egg yolks
75 g (3 oz) caster sugar
2 × 15 ml tbs cornflour
15 g (½ oz) butter

1 Roll out the pastry to a 23 × 30 (9 × 12 in) rectangle. Transfer to a dampened baking tray, prick the pastry all over with a fork and chill for 15 minutes. Bake at 220°C/425°F/Gas Mark 7 for 10-12 minutes until golden brown. Trim the edges of the rectangle, then cut widthways into three equal strips. Turn the strips over, return to the oven and bake for 5 minutes more. Cool on a wire rack.

2 To make the crème pâtissière, heat the milk with the vanilla pod in a heavy-based saucepan until almost boiling, then remove from the heat and leave to infuse for 30 minutes.

3 Whisk together the egg yolks and sugar until frothy, then whisk in the cornflour. Strain in the milk and whisk again. Return this mixture to the pan and cook over a low heat, stirring all the time, until boiling and thickened. Remove from the heat and beat in the butter. Cover the surface of the sauce with cling film and leave to cool.

4 Meanwhile, purée the raspberries in a blender and place in a saucepan with the redcurrant jelly. Place over a low heat and stir until the jelly has melted. Leave to cool, stirring occasionally, then stir in one-third of the strawberries. When the

crème pâtissière is cold, fold in the whipped double cream.

5 When ready to serve, spread the crème pâtissière over two strips of the pastry and carefully arrange half of the plain strawberries on top of each. Lay one strip on top of the other, then top with the final layer of pastry and spoon the fruit mixture on top to cover the pastry. Serve at once, decorated with strawberry leaves.

CAFE DESSERT

SERVES 6

300 ml (10 fl oz) double cream
1-2 × 15 ml tbs instant coffee powder
225 g (8 oz) fromage frais or other low-fat soft cheese
4 × 15 ml tbs brandy
115 g (4 oz) caster sugar
brandy snaps, to serve

1 Whip the cream with the coffee powder until the cream forms soft peaks and the coffee has dissolved. Fold the cream mixture into the cheese with the brandy and sugar.

2 Spoon the cream mixture into six tall glasses and serve at room temperature with brandy snaps.

Strawberry Mille Feuilles

ORANGE SLICES IN COINTREAU

MAKES ABOUT TWO 450 g (1 lb) JARS

335 g (12 oz) sugar
1.3 lt (2¼ pt) water
6 firm oranges, skins scrubbed clean
1 small cinnamon stick
1 × 5 ml tsp cloves
150 ml (5 fl oz) Cointreau

1 Put the sugar and 425 ml (15 fl oz) of the water in a saucepan. Heat gently until the sugar has dissolved, then bring to the boil. Boil for 1 minute, then add the remaining water.
2 Cut the oranges into 0.6 cm (¼ in) thick slices. Add the oranges and spices to the sugar syrup and poach gently for about 45 minutes, or until tender. Remove from the heat and drain, reserving the syrup; remove the cinnamon stick, if wished. Leave to cool for 30 minutes.
3 Arrange the fruit in sterilized jars, adding a few of the cloves. Add the liqueur to the remaining syrup and pour over the orange slices. Cover at once with airtight tops, label and leave to mature for at least 1 month.

DRIED FRUIT COMPOTE

SERVES 4

450 g (1 lb) mixed dried fruit
425 ml (15 fl oz) orange juice
150 ml (5 fl oz) water
300 ml (10 fl oz) medium dry white wine
2 × 15 ml tbs Cointreau

1 Place the fruit in a bowl and pour the orange juice and the water over the top. Cover and leave to soak overnight.

2 Transfer to a large saucepan, add the wine and Cointreau and bring to the boil. Cover and simmer gently for 45-50 minutes until the fruit is plump and very tender. Leave to cool before serving.

PEARS POACHED IN THREE WINES

SERVES 4

175 g (6 oz) sugar
350 ml (12 fl oz) water
150 ml (5 fl oz) each red, white and rosé wine
1 cinnamon stick
1 strip each orange and lemon rind
2 bay leaves
6 ripe William or Packham pears, peeled, halved and cored
bay leaves, to decorate

1 Divide the sugar among three saucepans and add 115 ml (4 fl oz) water to each. Pour the red wine into one with the cinnamon stick; the rosé in the second with the orange and lemon rind and the bay leaves and white wine in the third.
2 Place the pans over a low heat and stir each to dissolve the sugar, then bring each to the boil and boil for 2 minutes. Add four pear halves to each pan, cover and simmer gently for 10-15 minutes until just tender.
3 Remove the pears from the pans and transfer to a serving dish. Strain the syrups into one pan and boil hard for 3-5 minutes until syrupy. Finely shred the orange and lemon rind. Add to the syrup, then pour over the pears and leave to cool. Serve decorated with bay leaves.

COOK'S TIP

Using three different types of wine gives the dish a very attractive look, but if preferred you can always use just one type of wine.

TOP AND BOTTOM Orange slices in Cointreau
CENTRE Dried Fruit Compote

CREPES ANNETTE

SERVES 6

250 g (9 oz) plain flour
1 × 5 ml tsp baking powder
½ × 5 ml tsp bicarbonate of soda
pinch of salt
9 × 15 ml tbs kirsch
600 ml (20 fl oz) milk
25 g (1 oz) butter, melted
2 eggs, beaten
vegetable oil, for frying
560 g can red plums in syrup
175 g (6 oz) full fat soft cheese
50 g (2 oz) caster sugar
fresh mint, to decorate

1 To make the crêpes, sift the flour with the baking powder, soda and salt. Add 6 × 15 ml tbs kirsch with the milk, melted butter and eggs. Beat until smooth.

2 Heat a little oil in a heavy-based frying pan. Pour in 2 × 15 ml tbs batter. Swirl around pan and cook until golden underneath. Flip over and cook on the other side.

3 Turn the crêpe out on to a plate lined with greaseproof paper and keep warm. Repeat with the remaining batter to make twelve crêpes, stacking them with greaseproof paper in between each one. Keep warm.

4 Drain the plums, reserving the syrup. Stone the plums and set four aside. Chop the remaining plums. Beat the cheese and sugar until soft then fold in the chopped plums.

5 Spread a little filling on each crêpe and fold into triangles or roll up. Keep warm.

6 Cut the reserved plums into quarters lengthways. Heat the reserved syrup in a pan. Boil hard for 2 minutes to reduce by half. Stir in the plum quarters and heat through. Remove the plum quarters with a slotted spoon and tuck into the crêpes. Gently warm the remaining kirsch. Drizzle the hot plum syrup over the crêpes, then add the kirsch and set alight. Serve at once, decorated with fresh mint.

Crêpes Annette

CLAFOUTI

SERVES 4

3 × 15 ml tbs plain flour
pinch of salt
3 eggs, beaten
4 × 15 ml tbs caster sugar
450 ml (16 fl oz) milk
25 g (1 oz) butter
675 g (1½ lb) red cherries, stoned

1 Sift together the flour and salt into a bowl, then beat in the eggs and 3 × 15 ml tbs of the sugar. Heat the milk until almost boiling and beat into the egg mixture.

2 Butter a large, shallow ovenproof dish and add the cherries. Pour the batter over the top and dot with the remaining butter. Bake in the oven at 220°C/425°F/Gas Mark 7 for about 25 minutes until set and golden brown. Sprinkle the remaining caster sugar over the top and serve warm.

COOK'S TIP

This classic French dessert is also delicious made with well drained, canned pitted black cherries when fresh black cherries are out of season. Fresh Victoria plums, stoned and sliced, are also very good cooked this way.

Clafouti

HAZELNUT VACHERIN WITH APRICOTS

SERVES 6

115 g (4 oz) hazelnuts
3 egg whites
175 g (6 oz) caster sugar
½ × 5 ml tsp vanilla essence
50 g (2 oz) sugar
150 ml (5 fl oz) water
225 g (8 oz) fresh apricots, halved and stoned
grated rind of 1 lemon
150 ml (5 fl oz) double cream
sprigs of mint and fresh apricots, to decorate

1 Spread out the hazelnuts on a baking tray and grill, shaking frequently, until browned. Leave to cool completely, then finely chop with a sharp knife. (Do not chop in the food processor as this will make the meringue too oily.)

2 Whisk the egg whites until holding soft peaks, then whisk in half of the caster sugar, one spoonful at a time. Whisk for about 30 seconds until holding quite stiff peaks, then fold in the remaining caster sugar. Carefully fold in the hazelnuts with the vanilla essence.

3 Spoon the mixture into a large piping bag fitted with a 0.6 cm (¼ in) plain nozzle. Line two baking trays with non-stick baking paper and draw a 23 cm (9 in) circle on each.

4 Pipe the meringue in a spiral to make a complete round on each piece of paper.

5 Bake the meringue in the oven at 150°C/300°F/Gas Mark 2 for 40-50 minutes until dry and crisp. Leave to cool on the baking trays, then carefully peel off the paper.

6 While the meringues are cooling, place the remaining sugar in a pan with the water and place over a low heat. Stir until the sugar has dissolved, then add the apricots and lemon rind and simmer for 10 minutes until the apricots are just tender, yet still holding their shape.

7 Remove half of the apricots from the pan and set aside. Cook the rest for 5 minutes more until very soft, then drain (reserving the syrup) and push through a sieve to remove the skins. Allow to cool.

8 When ready to serve, spread half of the apricot purée over one meringue. Whip the cream to soft peak stage and carefully spread over the apricot purée. Arrange the reserved apricot halves on the cream, and place the remaining meringue round on top. Stir 3 × 15 ml tbs of the reserved syrup into the remaining apricot purée and serve as a sauce with the vacherin. Decorate the vacherin with sprigs of mint and fresh apricots.

COOK'S TIP

This elaborate dessert is made up of layers of hazelnut meringue which are sandwiched together with apricots and cream. The baked, unfilled meringue rounds keep well for up to two days, stored in an airtight tin. However, once the vacherin is assembled, it should be served within 30 minutes.

If wished, the apricot purée can be folded into the whipped cream to make a simple fool filling.

Hazelnut Vacherin with Apricots

INDEX